How to Draw Animals For Kids

Author Tony R. Smith

Copyright © 2019 by Tony R. Smith. All Rights Reserved.

No part of this publication may be reproduced, distributed, or transmitted in any form or by any means, including photocopying, recording, or other electronic or mechanical methods, or by any information storage and retrieval system without the prior written permission of Smith Show Publishing, except in the case of very brief quotations embodied in critical reviews and certain other noncommercial uses permitted by copyright law.

Example #1 Practice

Example of (Smudge Shading). Smudge Shading will give your drawing a complete look.

Example of (Tonal Shading). Tonal Shading will give your drawing a smooth contrast finish.

Example of (Light Smudge Shading). Light Smudge Shading will give your drawing a complete look.

Example of (Hatching Shading). Hatching Shading will help blend your drawing together.

Example #1 Final Drawing

Example #2 Practice

Example #2 Final Drawing

Practice

Practice

Practice

Practice

Practice

Practice

Practice

Practice

Practice

Practice

Practice

Practice

Practice

Practice

Practice

Practice

Practice

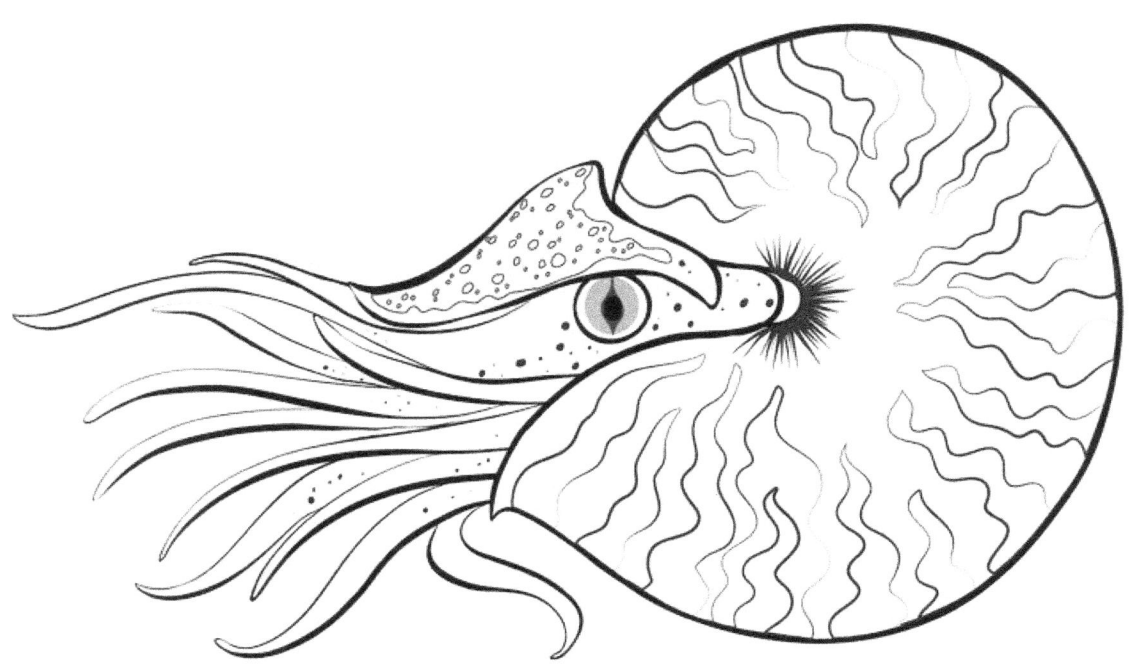

Practice

Practice

Practice

Practice

Practice

Practice

Practice

Practice

Practice

Practice

Practice

Practice

Practice

Practice

Practice

Practice

Practice

Practice

Practice

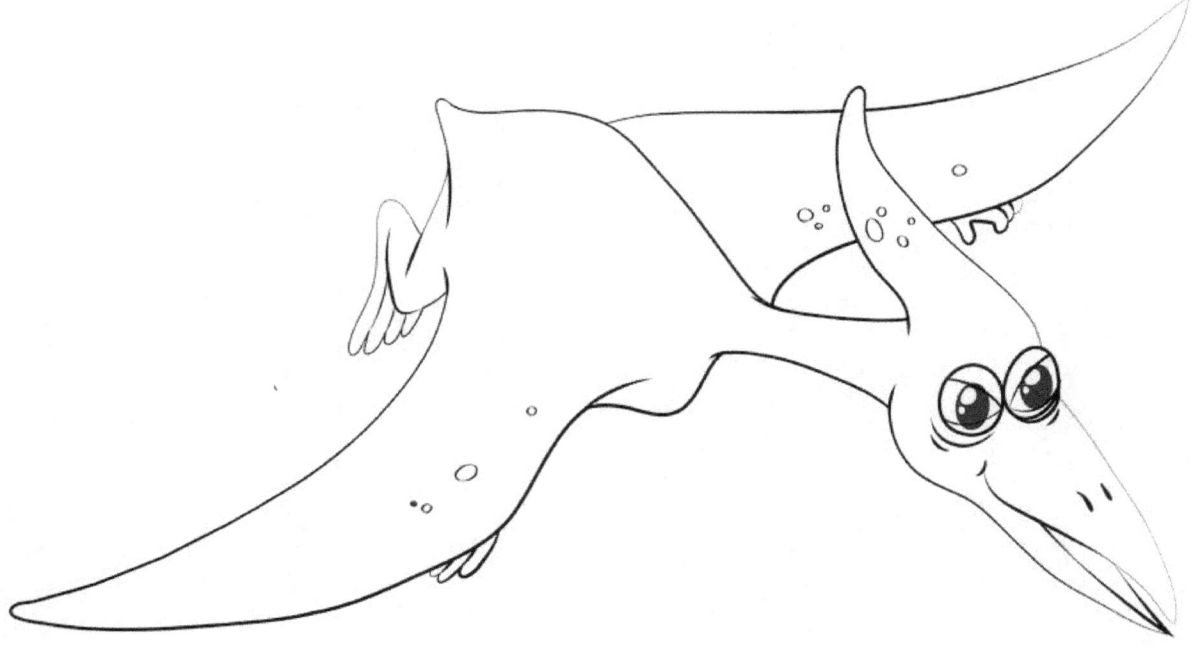

Practice

Practice

Practice

Practice

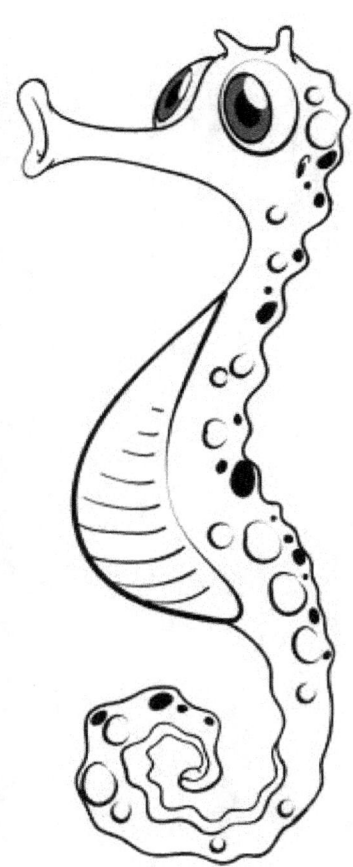

Practice

Practice

Practice

Practice

Practice

Practice

Practice

Practice

Practice

Disclaimer Statement

All information and content contained in this book are provided solely for general information and reference purposes. SSP LLC Limited makes no statement, representation, warranty or guarantee as to the accuracy, reliability or timeliness of the information and content contained in this Book.

Neither SSP Limited or the author of this book nor any of its related company accepts any responsibility or liability for any direct or indirect loss or damage (whether in tort, contract or otherwise) which may be suffered or occasioned by any person howsoever arising due to any inaccuracy, omission, misrepresentation or error in respect of any information and content provided by this book (including any third-party books.

www.ingramcontent.com/pod-product-compliance
Lightning Source LLC
Chambersburg PA
CBHW081753100526
44592CB00015B/2416